Spendaholics Anonymous

The Road from Six figures to the poverty line...and back again

by

Anna Martin

For Megan & Cameron

who believed their Mom wore her drawers on the outside of

her tights

and had a red cape...

at least for a little while!

All rights reserved

copy right 2018 Anna Martin

ISBN 9781731574992

Contents

Table of contents

1. Intro
2. Def-con Two
3. Entitled
4. Mindsets
5. Where do you start?
6. The "B" Word – budget!
7. The Art of False Economy
8. Food, Glorious Food
9. Tricks for stopping your overspending habit
10. Ways to lower those monthly bills
11. Your Credit Score
12. Gaining control over your money
13. Making more – The art of the Side Hustle
14. The State of the Nation

Resources

1.

Intro

Hi everyone. Welcome. Thanks for coming tonight. I'll start.... My name's Anna and I like to spend money.

I'm a Spendaholic and that's how I found myself $88,000 in debt and fired! Phew! Glad that's out of the way. Now it's your turn. How much debt are you carrying right now, today?

What? You don't know or your don't want to say it out loud? I hear you. Most people would rather discuss their sex lives in gory detail than talk about their failure with finance. Why is that? When did Debt become more Taboo than sex? When did we start lying about and hiding our debt levels from friends and family?

Debt is a disease – a silent killer, but we are more likely to share a fatal diagnosis than our credit card balances and the reason for that is Shame. Most of us are ashamed to admit we have No Money. It's the Elephant in the room. Everyone is ignoring it. The problem is, when you enter a room and everyone there has their own Elephant, that's claustrophobic, a "can't breathe" situation and everyone is suffocating.

2.

Def-con two

Have you seen the Debt clock on Wall street? I took a screenshot of the US Debt clock today – Oct 11th 2018.

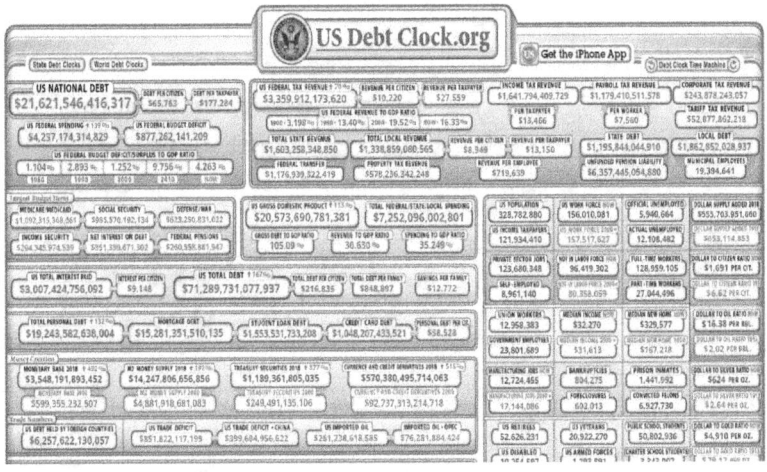

Check it out for yourself. This clock was ticking higher and higher at a rate of over $10,000 per second. The total US debt attributable to each US citizen was $216,835 and credit card debt stood at $1,048,207,433,521. I don't even know how to say that number...eleventy billion works just fine.

Ah! But that's the US.

You think Canada is better off?

CANADA'S FEDERAL DEBT

$  661,099,926,234.00

YOUR SHARE

$ 17,885.05

GROWTH OF DEBT PER DAY

$ 49,589,041.10

PER HOUR

$ 2,066,210.05

This is today and, by the time this book is published, the situation will be even worse. what's even more laughable is, this is the Federal clock. Each province of Canada has it's own Debt clock too.

Here's BC's.

Some time back I read an article in the Globe and Mail (Dec 2010) where the CEO of Canada's largest bank (RBC) was warning people not to rack up anymore debt. Considering that is the business he was in though, that's how he makes his money; What the hell?

The headline read "Ottawa in talks to rein in consumer debt". The government were actually looking to put measures into the Federal Budget to curb the rise of consumer debt.

In <u>2010</u> he was quoted as stating "We are clearly at the limit...". Back then the average debt per household, including mortgage and credit cards stood at $96,100. By 2012 it had climbed to over $100,000. At the end of 2017 Canadian households owed just over 2 trillion dollars (mortgages included) and by Q2 of 2018 total debt per household was $189,692. (stats Canada).

One day after the Globe and Mail published "Ottawa in talks..." the headline changed to "Debt Alert" and Canadians were urged NOT to use their credit cards to finance Christmas that year. The article noted (according to Stats Canada) that the average debt to income ratio of the average Canadian was 148.1 percent. Today that is 170.1 percent. (For every dollar earned, the average Canadian owes $1.70).

The Median debt (excluding mortgages) was circa $25,000. When I went down I had $88,000 of Debt, not including my mortgage! When I went down my household income was over $135,000 a year and had been more than $100,000 a year for a decade.

Does that seem ludicrous? It's quite normal, I assure you.

So, no one wants to admit that they are in trouble with debt but we all know that many people are. The total lack of open discussion about finances is dangerous and potentially lethal.

Why on Earth would we not open up and discuss these issues and potentially learn from others who have made all of the mistakes thereby enabling us to avoid all of the pitfalls?

3.

Entitled

I've always had a sense of entitlement, especially when I was feeling down. Buying something, even if I didn't need it, lifted me up momentarily (shoppers high) and, for a good while there, I could stave off the Low (shoppers remorse) for quite some time.

I LOVED to treat friends by picking up the Tab when we went out. Pretending that this was my way of thanking them when really I was just trying to buy their affection and their admiration.
I would indulge in an impulse at the cost of racking up more on the credit cards than I could already (ever) afford to repay and I would justify it to myself by focusing on the fact that I made GOOD money; and I worked hard; and I <u>DESERVED</u> it.

Where does that come from? The idea that you deserve something? Why do you deserve it? What makes you feel this way?

For me it stems back to an extremely poor upbringing. My Momma, bless her heart, trying to raise four kids alone and on Welfare (now there's a Woman who deserves something nice), she did the best she could with what she had and I never knew her to own a credit card back then. Of course, we didn't take vacations either so... what need is there for credit?

That might sound strange to you. Why am I equating Credit with vacations? Well, let me tell you a little of my story.

In 2010 I took my family on vacation to Disney in Orlando Florida, paid for on credit and it cost me $8400. In 2013 we went again and that time it was a little over $10,000. The last time we went was 2015 and we went all out. That trip was just over $15,000.

Now, you might think that I paid the $8400 back and then racked up a new bill for $10,000. You might think I then paid off that $10,000 and racked up a new bill for the $15,000.

If you did, you would be wrong.

In a little under 6 years I racked up almost $33,500 in debt just taking my kids on vacation.

Shocked? Or are you laughing at me, shaking your head and closing the book?

I wouldn't blame you. Sure, it would be easy to pretend I have been a model citizen, a shining light, pillar of the community but I'm no such sort. Sorry! Carbon based entity here and prone to every stupid mistake in the book. Just Like You!

I really don't believe you can write about debt and adequately convey the feeling of soul sucking, life crushing impotence unless you have been there, done that, bought the T-shirt.

I just told you a little about me and I'll share more as we go but, we are here to talk about you.

You're not perfect either are you? I mean, you just bought a book about over indulgent spending and how to get out of Debt and I'm thinking you wouldn't have done that if you weren't exactly like me!

So, what's your poison? Clothes? Gadgets? Being Flash?
It doesn't really matter. They're all the same. That's our happy place and going there feels great!

Stop me if you've heard this one.."The definition of insanity is doing the same thing over and over but expecting different results" or, how about "If you always do what you've always done you're gonna get what you've always got".
Classic!

The first thing we have to do to stop this cycle is **Define your relationship with money.**

How can you have a "relationship" with money

Isn't money something you just use? A means to an end? The route of All Evil?

No Dude! Money is a tool that wise people use to enjoy life whilst ensuring the safety and security of themselves and their loved ones, sometimes for generations to come.

Have you heard "A fool and his money are soon parted"? That's a gem is it not?

My relationship with money was very disdainful. I wanted money but couldn't keep hold of it. The more I earned, the more I spent; better car, bigger house, designer shoes (sigh). I used money and I abused money and consequently, money was not my friend. I've been living a life far beyond my means since my first (rich) boyfriend decades ago. I took this mentality and 10,000 GBP (British pounds) of debt into my marriage and I continued in this vein for over 25 years.

You might think I was unable to master money because I'm not financially educated. Well, try not to choke but.. I'm an accountant. A Financial controller no less and I have been since I qualified in Accountancy back in 1989 / 1990.

Now you're definitely laughing at me right? You're thinking "How on earth can this woman be a corporate F.C. and have gotten into so much trouble with money?" "Who on Earth would trust her with their finances?"

Judgy much!

I go back to the relationship with money. From the earliest of days (and I started making my own money at 14 years old – much to the chagrin of my School Principal), I was a spender. As soon as I could have a credit card I got one. I never paid off the balance in full and soon I struggled to make even the minimum payments. For decades I have paid thousands of pounds (and then dollars) in interest and my card holders? – They LOVED me! New card with lower fees – here ya go. Increased limit? No problem – let me just press a button here. I was what is known in the Credit world as a REVOLVER.

Are you picturing a revolving door now? OK, good – you have the right idea, and just for the sake of clarity, a revolver is someone with continuing revolving credit (a balance carried forward from month to month).

Want some simple math?

Lets just say your credit card has a balance of $10,000 and you carry that forward each month for one year. My interest rate used to be 19.9%APR so lets say 20%. In one year the card provider or bank would make $2000 off me (a 20% ROI!!!) and they had to do nothing for it. Don't you wish you could get a 20% return on your money?

More story?.... ok.

I specifically remember having to work away for an Audit and I knew I had nothing in my chequing account (payday was the end of the week) and my cards where maxed out. The hotel was asking for payment in advance and so I called home. My husband managed to borrow some money from his brother and in the meantime I went back to the Front Desk and explained I had to travel home and was extremely sorry (I think I gave them some BS about an "emergency") and begged them not to charge me as I hadn't actually checked in. They made no promises and, for the next three days I made a three hour drive each way and worked an 8 hour day each day. The money we borrowed covered the Gas I used to travel almost 300 miles in each direction, each day, for three days. I cried with shame all the way home.

I would like to say this was an "Unusual" situation for us but, it really wasn't.

Working as a Financial controller, when it comes to the corporations I work for ...there is no **Emotional Attachment** to that money. In fact, I don't see it as Real Money. It's just numbers on a spreadsheet and I am The Master of the Spreadsheet.

<u>My</u> money on the other hand, that's tangible. I can go to the bank and withdraw my money and hold it in my hand and exchange it for goods. The company's money though ...Flat line! It's not real. I can't touch it. I can't see it. I sure as shit can't withdraw it and spend it (shudder). Not that I ever would.

Working as an Auditor for Fraud investigation one chooses very early in life which side of the line one will walk and I firmly choose the path of honesty and integrity every time... I need to be able to sleep at night.

When it comes to Bean counting though, I can work miracles. I know where every penny is and what it's allocated against. I can forecast a cash flow to within mere dollars (not hundreds or even thousands). One forecast I did for a very beautiful resort here on the Island actually turned out to be $6 different to budget. That's SIX dollars. Not too shabby when you consider we were dealing with Christmas bookings and gift card sales.

Even at the height of my financial crisis I knew exactly what was coming in, where it was allocated and that I couldn't afford (insert latest frivolous purchase here) because of my awesome spreadsheets. That didn't stop me though. If I wanted something I usually got it and budget be damned! It's only in the last two years that I've been able to change my mindset and I owe a lot of that to my husband and to debt counselling.

Are you wondering about that first sentence in the intro? I stated I'd been fired and it would be remiss of me not to point out here that this wasn't a finance job (I was dabbling in Hotel Management and I SUCKED at that) and I didn't actually deserve what I got.... and that's all I'm going to say about that, as per my settlement agreement.

So – back to mindsets.

During my research over the last few years I read more and more from the musings of Robert Kiyosaki, Dave Ramsey, Bob Proctor and other such wealthy people and I devised a "free report" to entice readers to give me their email addresses. The free report was "Mindsets of the Wealthy" and I'll lay it out for you here.

Have you ever pondered why the Rich are so Rich and how they stay that way? An elite group (1%) of super wealthy people that the likes of you and I may never meet?

In my struggle to make it back from the brink I have researched and read, attended webinars and watched video's produced by the likes of Robert Kiyosaki (Rich Dad, Poor Dad); Anik Singal (Lurn Nation) and Warren Buffet. I have followed the advice of Dave Ramsey; Jeff Bezos; Mark Zuckerberg and many others; all of whom have one thing in common. They have money. A lot of it.

What I discovered (and I'm sure many other people have discovered this too) is that they all have a similar mindset and they follow similar paths. I also discovered that it's not rocket science. We can do it to but it takes change.

We have to change the way we view money and how we use it.

My aim is to give you the ten most common "Millionaire Habits".

Use them wisely :)

4.

Mindsets of the Worlds Wealthiest

1. Rich People... Don't save.

When I say they don't save, what I mean is, they don't save like we do. From an early age you are taught to do well in school, to go to university (or college), to get a good job, save for retirement and your kids education and consume, consume, consume.

Welcome to the Rat Race.

A rich person will save money only to have available funds to invest – we will get to investment later. They will invest first, save second and spend last and ONLY if they have accumulated the surplus required for the spend.

Rich people don't have an "I can't afford it" mentality. They look at the problem differently and ask "How can I afford it?" (Rich Dad, Poor Dad).

I found this fascinating article entitled "The Rich don't save- they borrow" from a blog in 2012 and a lot of it rings very true..

"The Rich don't save, they borrow"

I've been reading a lot of articles lately about ways to get out of debt, and I'm not impressed. Now, I'm not saying go out and buy a lot of crap, run up your credit cards, and go into near bankruptcy… I'll tell you though, if you want to be rich, you should be comfortable with debt.

There are two kinds of debt, often called "good" debt and "bad" debt. Good debt is the kind that puts money in your pocket (that means more money than it costs you, let me be clear on that) like the mortgage on a rental property. Bad debt is the kind that just costs you money sort of like a big screen TV you can't pay cash for.

Having no debt can be a good thing, if you want to remain at the same net worth. You're house is paid off, so are your cars and toys…but the equity is locked up, and not making you anything other that standard appreciation (or depreciation).

For every dollar you save in the banks, earning you less in interest than inflation and thus losing you money, represents a lot of money other people can use to make more money. The bank can lend out multiple dollars for every dollar they have stored in savings. I'll let you in on a little secret though, the banks want you to save because they make a lot of money off of your savings, it's good for the "little" guys to deposit their money at under 1% interest, that way the bank can lend out 10 times that (or more/less depending on the economy) and charge 3-6%…

Imagine, you give the bank $100, they agree to pay you 1%, so $1/year (which, if you're in the highest tax bracket will cost you nearly 50 cents in taxes). The bank meanwhile can lend out $1,000 at let's say 5%, making them $50 on your $100.

Are they ripping you off? No. They are providing a service, and using the rules to make money. If you want a slice of the pie, buy some bank stocks or…

Do what the rich do.

When a wealthy person buys an investment, they rarely pay for it with their own money, they borrow money to pay for it. They leverage their net worth to make money. For example, if you owned your house worth $100,000, you'd have a tough time increasing the value of the house to $200,000 without spending money. If however, you borrowed $90,000 against the title of your house, bought 9 rental properties worth $100,000 each, you'd still be in the same situation as far as your net worth was concerned. You still only have a net worth of $100,000 but now control $1,000,000 worth of real estate (meaning if you sold everything you'd still only have $100,000 not $1,000,000 because you'd have to repay the bank the other $900,000 you borrowed).

Let's say your mortgage interest was 5% amortized over 25 years, making your payments about $525/month, and you could rent the place for $1,000/month. This means you're making $475 x 9 rentals x 12 months $45,900 each year. With taxes eating half, you could still double your net worth in just over 4 years.

This example is extremely simplified, for example there are other costs involved (lawyers, taxes, insurance, etc.) but on the flip side, if you were to reinvest your profits your taxes would be lower and your net worth would grow much quicker.

Even if you had the cash, I wouldn't recommend using more than the bear minimum, as you lock up it's earning power and put it at risk.

When the rich buy businesses, real estate, even stocks, they borrow money to do it, they get grants, subsidies, whatever. They use leverage to keep money working for them. The savers power them.

Now, this isn't meant to say go out and leverage everything to buy crap. You need to be smart, and buy smart. You have to make more money than you pay for that money, otherwise you've got "bad" debt.

"Bad" debt makes you poor, it doesn't matter if it's a big screen TV or a bad investment property.

There is no path that will make you money for nothing, but it's not difficult to make money either if you're willing to work. Saving isn't the path to wealth, and the system isn't corrupt.

If I had $50, would you be upset if I invested and turned it into $100? Would I be a bad person for doing that (assuming it was legal of course)? Would it be different if I used the same technique on $500? $5000? Then why does it change when you have a lot of money? In fact, it's more work to change $500,000 into $1,000,000 and riskier to boot, but it's the same return on investment. It's the same as 10,000 people changing $50 into $100, when you put aside taxes and probably employment. Don't get mad at people's success, just get off the couch and imitate them.

I often wonder why we listen to people who work for a pay check when it comes to investing. The people working for the banks, the magazines, the investment companies don't make money doing what they tell you to do, they make money by telling you what to do which makes their employer money.

If you want to be rich, look at how the wealthy make their money. Let me know if you ever read an article about Warren Buffet, Donald Trump, or anyone who "dipped" into their pocket and paid for a purchase outright. It doesn't happen in investing.

Lesson: Spent money is dead money, and dead money can't make you anything.

Source: http://www.easysafemoney.com

What did you think of that?

Following on from one of my favourite mentors – here's what Robert Kiyosaki has to say about the subject:-

"Savers are losers....

The traditional financial advice to save your money is a popular one. And maybe for an athlete making millions of dollars a year, it makes sense. But for the vast majority of people, saving is not a way to get rich or stay rich.

In fact, for the vast majority of people, saving is a sure fire way to lose. Why? Because inflation often rises higher than the interest rates you're paid for your money. So the whole time it's sitting in your bank account, it's actually losing money.

What's worse, money is a currency. If it doesn't keep moving, it dies. One sad thing about savers is that they never put their money to work for them, and because of this, they don't become rich.

This is why rather than teach people to be savers, I teach them to be spenders—in the right way."

> "It's important to note that saving does not equal paying yourself first. I've written a lot about why savers are losers. If you simply save money each month, you will never get ahead financially.
>
> Rather, you must save with a purpose. Both Kim and I have some savings set aside in the form of liquid assets like cash, gold, and silver, which we can use in an emergency. But the majority of our money goes into saving for investing into cash-flowing assets. It is these cash-flowing assets that then put money into our pockets each month. And it is cash-flowing assets—i.e., money working for you—that gets you out of the rat race."

Shocking Right – how can I be a loser if I have saved $1000 in my emergency fund?

Here's where we start changing your mindset. Ten ways the Rich think and act differently from you or I and what we need to adopt if we're going to be like them.

2. Rich People... Make money work for *them*.

Here's the kooky bit. We go out to work to make money. Rich people go out to make money work for them!

Rich people diversify and usually have multiple income streams earning them profits whilst they sleep.

I've been studying with Anik Singal – CEO of Lurn.com and he has a lot to say on multiple income streams:

> "Rich people buy assets (ie things that increase in value, provide an income, or preferably both).

Poor people buy bling. The basic concept of bling is "look at me, I've got more money than sense".

So, rich people invest in things they think will increase in value over the long term. Stocks, bonds, and real estate are the most common. Sometimes they will borrow to buy such assets, leveraging themselves, and increasing their return percentages.

Hopefully, things work out as they had planned. It is nice to get paid without having to get out of bed, having to punch a time clock!"

The rules of work have changed.

Most likely you're working *"for"* money, meaning you're selling your time in exchange for money.

This is called earned income.

To better illustrate this, earned income is like a farmer working with his hands. His production efficiency ratio is 1:1 = **ZERO leverage.**

It's extremely difficult to achieve financial freedom with earned income.

1. Earned income is the most heavily taxed source of income.

2. Earned income pays taxes BEFORE expenses.

3. Most probably your expenses are not allowing you to invest any money to accumulate wealth.

To increase your income, you need to use some kind of **leverage.**

The better the leverage, the more effective your hours of work will be.

Back to the farmer example:

With the use of a tool (*leverage*) the farmer above can produce 5X times more '*value*' during the same hours of work.

Now, the farmer is using not only a tool, but also the power of animals (increased leverage) to boost production.

This farmer can now produce 500X times more '*value*' during the same working hours.

Stop chasing money and start chasing value.

Reevaluate your work and daily actions. Think how you could be leveraging some skill, knowledge or tools.

3. Rich People... Build Assets

If I had to guess I'll bet you consider your house an Asset right?

WRONG!

We have been indoctrinated into the mindset that owning a property means you have added an asset to your portfolio. (I'm assuming here that the property is mortgage free).

Although you live in your property, It DOESN'T Pay you. It costs you. If it costs you any money at all – It's a liability. *"The key to financial success is understanding the relationship between the income statement and the balance sheet"* – Robert Kiyosaki.

The magic words are cash flow

It's this simple insight that explains why those with a low financial IQ are still poor even when they make more than $100,000 a year. They don't know how to move their money into assets that make them more money. Instead, they spend it all on liabilities and live large paycheck to large paycheck.

If you can understand the following diagrams, you have a better chance of acquiring great wealth.

~ *taken from Rich Dad: Poor Dad by Robert Kiyosaki. A recommended read!*

Cash flow patterns

An asset is something that puts money in your pocket. It's that simple. This is the cash-flow pattern of an asset:

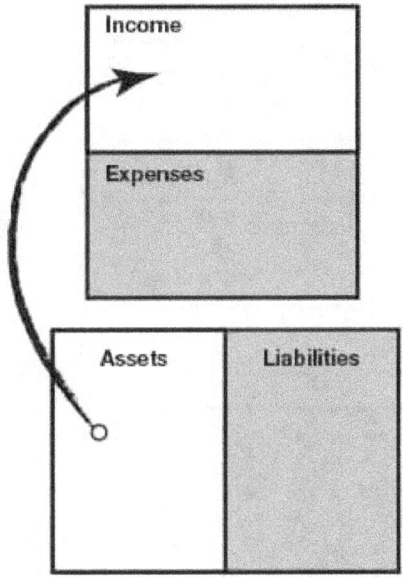

A liability is something that takes money out of your pocket.

This is the cash-flow pattern of a liability:

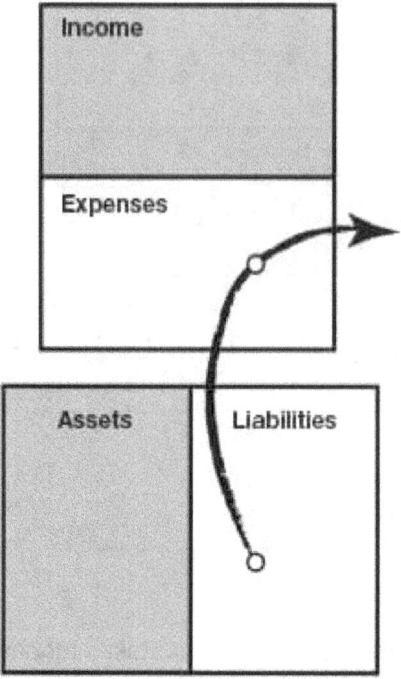

Where it gets confusing

Confusion happens for many because accepted methods of accounting allow for the listing of both assets and liabilities under the asset column.

To explain this, he again drew a simple diagram:

BALANCE SHEET

Assets	Liabilities
$100,000 House	$80,000 Mortgage

"This is why things get confusing," rich dad would say. "In this diagram, we have a $100,000 house where someone has put $20,000 cash down and now has an $80,000 mortgage. How do you know if this house is an asset or a liability? Is the house an asset just because it is listed under the asset column?"

The answer is, of course, no. In order to know for sure, you would need to refer to the income statement to see if it was an asset or a liability.

The house as a liability

To illustrate this, rich dad drew this diagram:

INCOME STATEMENT

Income

Expenses
Mortgage payment
Real estate taxes
Insurance
Utilities
Maintenance

BALANCE SHEET

Assets	Liabilities
$100,000 House	$80,000 Mortgage

"This is a house that is a liability," said rich dad. "You can tell it is a liability because it's only line items are under the expense column. Nothing is in the income column."

The house as an asset

Rich dad then added to the diagram a line that read "rental income" and "net rental income," the key word being "net." That addition to the financial statement changed that house from a liability to an asset.

```
┌─────────────────────────┐
│ Income                  │
│                         │
│         Rental income   │
│                         │
├─────────────────────────┤
│ Expenses                │
│        Mortgage payment │
│        Real estate taxes│
│        Insurance        │
│        Utilities        │
│        Maintenance      │
└─────────────────────────┘
```

Rental income — Expenses = Net rental income

Assets	Liabilities
🏠 $100,000 House	$80,000 Mortgage

These simple lessons are profound. And they are the basis for building all great wealth

Understanding the relationship between the income statement and the balance sheet allows you to quickly understand if an investment is an asset or a liability—and this understanding will allow you to make the right investment every time.

4. Rich People..Invest

Today's RICH invest three ways:

1. In income producing Assets;

2. First BEFORE spending;

3. In themselves. Education is KEY!

The wealthy have greater exposure to real estate and alternate investments in their portfolios.

A typical portfolio breakdown would be 25 per cent real estate – excluding their personal residences – plus 10 per cent alternative investments such as hedge funds, derivatives, foreign currency and private equity. Then a third of the portfolio consists of cash and fixed-income vehicles, and the balance is in equities.

People with a higher net worth tend to be more comfortable with those non-traditional, alternative ways of investing. They have invested in private equity through personally held corporations; that's how they earned a living.

Wealthy people see diversification differently.

"People who are very wealthy diversify their assets, but not in the sense of, 'Oh, I'm in stocks in China, India, Japan and Europe.' The general public diversifies in the stock market by buying other areas, whereas wealthy people diversify by being in a different asset class,".

> They own the debt market, even though the debt market doesn't pay them very much. It diversifies their equity risk – and I think this is where many people have got this very wrong, but wealthy people understand it. Yes, I can have a 2-per-cent rate of return and I'm not going to get more out of the bond market than that, but the money is less volatile and it's always there.

"History shows us that when the stock market falls, the bond market goes up. And vice versa. They are negatively correlated, whereas stock markets around the world are positively correlated. So somebody in the stock market, if they believe that the market is going to drop, they don't mind being in the bond market at 2 per cent. It allows them to make an asset-allocation change later when the stock market falls."

> Wealthy people often hold alternative investments such as real estate, private equity and hedge funds, but real estate doesn't mean they have to go buy property. They also can invest through financial markets in real estate exposure.

"They also invest in private companies, through private equity funds, funds that invest in, and/or buy, private companies. They also structure their portfolios by adding investments that protect it. For example, certain funds are used for hedging against a decline in the stock or bond market, while others are currency-hedged so that they can protect against fluctuations in the rise or fall of the dollar.

"That's the luxury the wealthy have, because they don't need the cash. They're not spending everything they make. They have the opportunity to think longer term. It's about time in the market, not timing of the market."

5. Rich People….Are FRUGAL

Warren Edward Buffett is an American business magnate, investor, and philanthropist who serves as the chairman and CEO of Berkshire Hathaway.

Net worth: 81.9 billion USD (2018) Forbes,

WOW!

>He lives in the same home he bought in 1958

It's **a five-bedroom** in central Omaha that he bought for $31,500, or about $260,000 in today's dollars.

If you want to be Buffett's neighbour, the house across the street will cost you **about $2.15 million.**

He never spends more than $3.17 on breakfast

On his five-minute drive to the office, which he's been doing for the past 54 years, **Buffett stops at McDonald's.**

Depending on how prosperous he's feeling, he orders one of three items: two sausage patties for $2.61, a sausage, egg and cheese for $2.95 or a bacon, egg and cheese for $3.17.

Despite his billions, he's a careful investor

Whether you love or hate the Facebook founder, everyone can agree that Mark Zuckerberg is one of the top frugal billionaires around. At a $40.7 billion net worth, Zuckerberg is worth over 100 Kardashian families (that's right, the whole family 100 times over and still have over $1 billion in his pocket). Although Zuckerberg is rolling in the dough, his lifestyle emulates a lifestyle closer to the average Joe.

He Dresses Simple:

If you notice one thing about this young billionaire it is that he wears the same style of outfit everyday. He wears the same grey t-shirt, jeans, and hoodie. His entire wardrobe probably costs less than $700, and it probably costs less than $200 a year to keep his wardrobe updated. Considering that the average American family spends around $1,700 a year on clothing, Zuckerberg definitely has the right idea on saving money.

He Drives Simple:

What do most super-wealthy individuals drive around in? Soccer superstar, David Beckham, has been seen driving his family around in a $407,000 Rolls-Royce Phantom Drophead. Zuckerberg drives a modest, black Acura TSX. This car costs a modest $30,000.

When the average non-wealthy person receives an unexpected windfall – They *SPEND* it!
"Hey Honey, I just got a tax refund. Let's take a vacation!" This was me. Is it you?

Rich people don't do this, they sacrifice. Vacations are put on hold until such a time as their assets earn enough to have the surplus available to spend without diminishing the worth of their portfolios.

6. Rich People… have goals, a strategy: AN ACTION Plan

> Top-level athletes, successful business people and achievers in all fields all set goals. Setting goals gives you long-term vision and short-term **motivation**. It focuses your acquisition of knowledge, and helps you to organize your time and your resources so that you can make the most of your life.

By setting sharp, clearly defined goals, you can measure and take pride in the achievement of those goals, and you'll see forward progress in what might previously have seemed a long pointless grind. You will also raise your **self-confidence**, as you recognize your own ability and competence in achieving the goals that you've set

How to Set a Goal

First consider what you want to achieve, and then commit to it. Set SMART (specific, measurable, attainable, relevant and time-bound) goals that motivate you and write them down to make them feel tangible. Then plan the steps you must take to realize your goal, and cross off each one as you work through them.

> Goal setting is a powerful process for thinking about your ideal future, and for motivating yourself to turn your vision of this future into reality.

The process of setting goals helps you choose where you want to go in life. By knowing precisely what you want to achieve, you know where you have to concentrate your efforts. You'll also quickly spot the distractions that can, so easily, lead you astray.

7. Rich People... understand Longevity

Do you ever think for one second that a Rich person would ever sign up for a "Get Rich (er) quick scheme"?

Play the long game.

To make money, an investor shouldn't buy a stock with the sole intention of selling. You're in it for the long game.

> "Our favourite holding period is forever," Buffett first said in a 1988 shareholders' letter.
>
> Buffett only buys stocks of companies he understands and likes, and thinks selling should be done when you need the money and not when you believe it is a strategic jumping off point.
>
> Rather than focusing on obstacles like most people tend to do, rich people focus, and capitalize, on opportunities.

Rich people see potential growth. Poor people see potential loss. Rich people focus on the rewards. Poor people focus on the risks.

Work toward long-term, not short-term goals.

Long-term goals take a minimum of one to five years to accomplish. Long-term goals are excellent motivators. They enable you to look beyond the moment and put into perspective why you are spending your time today as you are.

Understand the best goals play out over time, not spontaneously.

The rich understand that the best goals play out over time. They don't happen spontaneously. Goal setting is an ongoing activity. The rich know that they need to remind themselves to stay on track. The rich don't write down their goals and put them away. They make regular appointments on their calendars to review their goals.

The destination for long-term goals may not seem to change but the steps they take to get there will. No matter whether your long-term goal will take five or 20 years, remember that the journey takes time. Keep moving forward, knowing that over time you must attain your goals.

Of course, the easiest way to play a really Long Game is to Start Early!

8. Rich People… associate with like minds

Rich people think and act differently than the rest of us. They aren't born with this "rich mentality" — they learn how and then choose to think and act this way. **Rich people choose to hang out with other rich people** The rich associate with those who are equally or more rich.

Successful people look at other successful people as a means to motivate themselves. They see other successful people as models to learn from. They say to themselves, 'If they can do it, I can do it.'

Rather than being jealous of other successful people, they are grateful for them, as they provide a template for how to attain such success.

The fastest and easiest way to create wealth is to learn exactly how rich people, who are masters of money, play the game.

Did you know that many of the world's most famous entrepreneurs have mentors? They understand that success is not a one-person show and that mentors can help keep their businesses innovative and relevant. Entrepreneurs with mentors show that they are willing to learn, open to different perspectives and adaptable to change.

"A SMALL AMOUNT OF TIME INVESTED ON YOUR PART TO SHARE YOUR EXPERTISE CAN OPEN UP A NEW WORLD FOR SOMEONE ELSE." – MARK ZUCKERBERG

Zuckerberg talked about his inspiring mentor Steve Jobs. "He was amazing, I had a lot of questions for him." He described how Jobs gave him advice about how he could build a team that was as focused as Zuckerberg on building "high quality and good things". They also both believed that their life paths were meant for more than just building businesses. They wanted to change the lives of people.

"AS WE LOOK AHEAD INTO THE NEXT CENTURY, LEADERS WILL BE THOSE WHO EMPOWER OTHERS." – BILL GATES

Bill Gates is currently listed as the richest person in the world. The Harvard drop-out credits part of his success to his mentor, businessman and investor, Warren Buffet.

"IF YOU ASK ANY SUCCESSFUL BUSINESSPERSON, THEY WILL ALWAYS (SAY THEY) HAVE HAD A GREAT MENTOR AT SOME POINT ALONG THE ROAD." – RICHARD BRANSON

Branson believes the first step to finding a great mentor is admitting you can benefit from a mentor: Going it alone is an admirable, but foolhardy and highly flawed approach to taking on the world.

Right now I am being mentored by Anik Singal and his team and following Robert Kiyosaki's philosophies in changing my relationship with money.

9. Rich People... take calculated risks

> Wealthy people are not any smarter than poor people; they just have different and more supportive money habits. The single biggest difference between financial success and financial failure is how well you manage your money. It's simple: to master money, you must manage money.

Average people choose not to manage their money because they believe they don't have enough to manage.

Until you show you can handle what you've got, you won't get any more! The habit of managing your money is more important than the amount.

I won't say that Rich people never gamble, that's silly. They make wagers on all kinds of things but, do you think they buy a lotto ticket every Friday in the vain hope that the money Gods will shine their light upon them? Pfft – No.

Rich people choose to constantly learn and grow.

The wealthiest learn how to be successful from those who are richer and more successful than they are. They then continue to learn even after they've attained incredible success.

"Every master was once a disaster," No one comes out of the womb a financial genius. Every rich person learned how to succeed at the money game, and so can you ... Success is a learnable skill."

10. Rich People… embrace failure

Most people don't even try because they don't want to fail. Do you honestly believe that all of those self made, entrepreneurial millionaires didn't fail, at least once?

Thomas A. **Edison quotes** "I have not **failed**. I've just found 10,000 ways that won't work." Many of life's **"failures"** are people who did not realize how close they were to success when they gave up.

Sometimes a failure might just be the best thing that ever happened to you.

When I lost my job and my husband lost his, *In The Same Week*, we were lost. We felt like total failures.

Looking back now. If I was still employed I would still be working 24/7 (literally), still not have taken a relaxing vacation (in five years) and would still be almost $100,000 in debt, if not more! I would have felt guilty taking a day off to see my daughter graduate and would have been fighting fires for a week after taking one day off.

My husband would probably be dead. That's no joke. It's taken two years to bring his health back from that brink.

> Successful people will tell you they have failed. That, in fact, they have failed many times. The difference between these high achievers and the rest of us is that even though we all may reflexively regurgitate the same clichés about failing and the value of lessons learned, successful people actually believe them in a substantially deeper manner.

I have consistently observed that those in the top tier of **success** don't internalize failure in the same way that most people do. For them, failure is not a reflection of self. It is completely objectified and isolated, believed to be an experience from which to learn, a measure of the inability to accomplish one specific task at a single moment in time, or the result of variables that likely have little to do with the individual in question. Nothing more.

Mindset Conclusion

WHY are the Rich, Rich?

In a country like ours, with the opportunities that we have, why is it that so few people retire financially independent?

First, at the top of the list, is that it never occurs to them.

The average person has grown up in a family where he has never met or known anyone who was wealthy. He goes to school and socializes with people who are not wealthy. He works with people who are not wealthy. He has a reference group or a social circle outside of work who are not wealthy. He has no role models who are wealthy.

If this has happened to you throughout your formative years, up to the age of twenty, you can grow up and become a fully mature adult in our society, and it may never occur to you that it's just as possible for you to become wealthy as for anyone else. My kids? They go to a private school, alongside Hollywood Actors and Eminent Doctors Kids. They have enough funds to go onto college without thinking about how they will pay for it. My daughter will travel for her Gap year and she won't think twice about visiting a museum or a Castle – to see if that's in the budget.

Please don't think we handed them this life on a platter. My daughter has worked since she was 14 and her Gap year is self financed. Our investments have enabled us to give them their education and, even when we hit rock bottom, I paid the school first and the mortgage second and I don't regret a second of it. That's because I carry no shame in being able to now say to people "No, I can't afford that."

5.

Where do you start?

Are you kidding me? You've already started! You bought this book. You made it through almost 30 pages of how to think like a Rich person. What's left is straightforward. Child's play even.

Our story...

I would like to take this opportunity to talk about **how I got out** and, whilst it's not for everyone, It was right for me.

When my husband and I entered into what we now call our "Personal Economic Collapse" we did the right thing. We called every creditor on DAY TWO (we called the lawyers on Day One!) and explained the situation and asked what our options where. Do you know what we got? From our Bank of 10 years (CIBC)? From the car loan bank (RBC)? From Visa? From Mastercard? From Amex? They all said the same thing..

TOO BAD. SUCKS TO BE YOU. WHEN ARE YOU GOING TO PAY US?

We consulted our lawyer and we tried again two weeks later, to negotiate halting our payments and we also enacted every single insurance policy we had. Do you know what we found out? Those insurance policies aren't worth the damn paper they're written on.

Pretty soon we had collection agents calling and threatening letters arriving and the stress levels rose exponentially.

Neither of us were sleeping worth a damn and I was terrified we would lose the house or the kids school money. A lien was placed on the house and on the truck and at any moment the whole house of cards was about to cave in.

One day I came home from my new job (earning 50% less than I previously made) to find out that my husband had contacted a credit counselling agency and that we had an appointment later that week.

Given that I was still living in denial of our predicament, I was not pleased that he had done this without first speaking with me.

After that initial meeting with Sue Grubac from 4 Pillars (https://www.4pillars.ca/) I was reeling. I wasn't happy at all but, at the same time, I was blanking out the situation and its gory details and leaving my husband to deal with it all by himself.

At the meeting we were given our options and plans were outlined and we were told, in detail, what we could expect to see happen and what it would mean to us. Best of all – We were NOT JUDGED.

We opted for a Consumer Proposal. Less scary than a full Bankruptcy but more robust than a debt Management Program.

So, whats the difference?

Credit counselling: Debt Management Program (DMP)

This generally involves making contact with all of your creditors to negotiate a plan to pay off 100% of your debt. Usually, the creditors agree to stop charging interest that is accruing on the principal in exchange for getting the principal back.

A DMP is designed for people who can afford to pay off all of their debts over a period of time, but are not able to get a debt consolidation loan. It works because the credit counselling agency contact the creditors on your behalf (which shows them you have sought professional help) and they will coordinate the payments to the creditors on your behalf. You make one Monthly payment to the agency. This is what we tried to day in the early days but without the benefit of professional backing.

The agency places your monthly payment into a Trust account and then makes a proportional payment to each creditor on the list.

Pro's: Interest stops accumulating; creditor calls stop; it's voluntary; one monthly payment is simple to remember and easy to budget for.

Cons: it doesn't have to include all of your creditors; it is not binding on the creditors who agree to negotiate with you; there's no time limit to the length of the plan.

Consumer Proposal (CP)

A CP is a negotiated offer to all of your creditors (for unsecured debt) to pay back a portion of what you owe them over a predetermined period of time – say three to five years (max). It is an alternative to bankruptcy and must be administered by a licensed bankruptcy trustee. This might be your best option if your debts are between $5,000 and $250,000, excluding mortgage; you can't get a consolidation loan; you are employed or have a source of income that allows you to make monthly payments; you can't afford to pay 100% of your debts back; you want to avoid losing your home so bankruptcy is OUT!

Pro's: you can negotiate to pay less than 100% of what you owe; Creditor calls and wage garnishments stop; interest charges stop; you don't lose your house OR Any Other Assets (this was especially important to us as our daughter was 16 and her RESP was crucial for school); the negative effect on your credit rating is less severe than bankruptcy; the maximum repayment period is five years. You can repay early in the event of a sudden windfall (like a settlement agreement from a Labour case or an inheritance or tax refund, etc) and it will enable you to pick up your credit scores that much sooner.

Creditors have 45 days to vote on the proposal, which has to be accepted by all parties if if the majority (over 50%) vote in favour of acceptance. Creditors will usually pick this option if they will get more back than if you were declared bankrupt.

Cons: You cannot pick and choose which debts to include and it does not cover secured debt.

<u>Bankruptcy</u>

This is generally classed as a last resort but for some it may be there best option. Filing for bankruptcy is for those who have no alternatives because their debt levels are just too high. In this instance you must work with a Licensed professional who will attempt to sell off any assets you may own and will hold the proceeds in trust. You will get to keep any RRSP you may hold (with the exemption of the last 12 months of payments) and a certain amount of furniture, tools of your trade and some life policies. If your vehicle is worth less than the deminimus limit (approx $6,000) you may be allowed to keep that too.

Pro's: If all goes well you are discharged from being a Bankrupt nine months after filing (24 months if this is your second strike).

This was just a brief overview of options. Please seek professional advice from a counsellor or Licensed Trustee. We wholly endorse 4Pillars Credit Counselling agency. www.4pillars.com.

Our story....continued

Once we signed on the dotted line and the negotiations started on our behalf there was a definite shift in the atmosphere at home.

The counsellors and lawyers involved kept us in the loop the whole time and we started our credit counselling to ensure this didn't happen to us again.

On one of our last visits Sue came to us and said "I have news and you're not going to believe it." Obviously I almost threw up, expecting the worse but she just smiled and said "I've never seen this, in all my years in this business."

One of the creditors had made a fundamental mistake in their calculations and, instead of putting in for $41,000, they asked for $14,000. Our lawyers gave them three opportunities to correct their error before the final contract negotiation date and each time, they missed it.

When the dust settled and our five year plan was ratified and filed with the courts we only needed to pay $16,000 in cash (there's a 25% discount for early settlement) and our truck was worth at least $20,000. My husband immediately got to work in exchanging the truck for cash and a small car (no finance involved) – A Big shout out and Thank you to the amazing staff at Finneron Hyundai – and within weeks we were clear.

No debt. No 5 year payment plan. Nothing – ALL GONE.

Was that a Miracle? It was certainly fortuitous and I thank my lucky stars every day. My friends say it's justice because what happened to us was disgusting. The man responsible for our PEC (personal economic collapse) should be boiled in oil.

To him, I say Thank you. Sincerely, thank you.

Without your heinous act and without my wonderful lawyers and counsellors I could still be working for you. Dying just a little more inside each and every day. Instead, I greet each new day with joy. My family is strong and happy and my husband is alive and well. Flourishing actually.

I've learned to live on less and my life is more fulfilled because of it. My friends have a "real" person to hang with and not a false shell. My family has a happy, loving Mother / Wife and we want for nothing...well, almost nothing.

OK, enough about me.

Let's look at <u>step one</u>. Assessing your finances and building a budget together shall we?

6.

The "B" Word...Budget!

What is this and How to create one.

The challenges of getting your bills paid on time each may be huge. It's ideal to find ways to help you do so and to work on a budget could be your best defence. This will allow you to know where your money is going on a regular basis and may just be the help you need to avoid overspending. Starting a budget is difficult, but will take some effort and commitment on your part to stick to it. By knowing specific tips to assist you in creating a monthly budget, this may encourage you to begin.

1. Make a list

The first thing you should do is to create a list of your bills each month. This will allow you to know how much money you owe to your creditors. Be sure to include all of your expenses from your house payment or rent to the cars you own. There are numerous other costs you may be forced to pay each month and these range from grocery bills to gasoline to get your where you need to go. Don't forget to add your auto and health insurance and any miscellaneous expenses, as well.

Knowing the amount, you owe monthly, and the date your payments are due is the first step in creating a budget.

Stay on track

You will want to _heed your budget_ once you've made it. This means sticking to the things you have written down and not spending a lot of money on things that you don't need. I was great at maintaining my budget on the spreadsheets but awful at commitment.

It's ideal to include some money for entertainment purposes, such as going out to dinner or watching a movie with friends. Adding these small things can help you work harder and even be more likely to stick to your budget. All work and No play.... you get my meaning?

You will have greater control over your financial situation by making a budget and sticking to it as much as possible. Doing so may be the assistance you need to avoid financial pitfalls that could prevent you from getting any and all of your bills paid promptly.

Six Simple (Very Simple) Secrets of Budgeting Your Bills

The number one secret is to open all your bills. Too simple for you? Not at all. It's only human nature to avoid bad news, but not opening a bill can lead to an even more unpleasant surprise: late fees.

So always avoiding late fees is your first step. So far, not too difficult, is it? The other steps here are not complicated either and, if these ideas do not work for you, our final suggestion should be sure to your liking.

More on that later.

Meanwhile:

2. Let's face it. You hate budgeting. It's like opening your bills - very unpleasant. But like death and taxes, it is a necessity. There's nothing really complicated here either. Add up all your bills. Figure out what you owe and what is left over is for you to spend foolishly or not. It's pretty simple and it doesn't take much effort if you get used to doing it.

3. Find a place for your bills. This also sounds elementary but consider that it is likely your income or incomes are paid weekly or twice a month. Bills tend to come monthly.
So you need to organize those bills into some sensible system. This does not require a huge office but perhaps simply an accordion folder for financial papers with tabs on when a bill has to be paid. Establish your own home financial centre.

4. This brings us to set up regular times to pay bills. It might be once a month, once a week or once a day. Make that a quiet time. Get in as peaceful a mood as you can when facing this obvious obstacle (this is not easy but try). You want to be as relaxed as possible. However you pay your bills, make your system is simple. A simple filing system and regular payments will ensure you pay every bill on time.

5. Look at when to pay. Everything can be changed. Find the most convenient time for you to pay. Notify your creditors and ask for that time. You probably hate to call or notify creditors of anything, but try it anyway. If you get paid on the 5th of the month but your bills are scheduled to leave on the 1st, it's a no brainer to call and request a pay date that falls shortly after you get paid.

6. If all of this is too confusing or difficult, consider using an online service. If you need something more high-tech than an accordion file and are stumped about how to best organize your bills, there are plenty of websites and apps that promise to do just that. These include FileThis.com; Finovera.com; Check.me; and MoneyStream.com.
All are low-cost or even free.

What does a Simple Budget look like?
Like I said, I'm the queen of the Spreadsheets so here's my ACTUAL monthly budget.

	October	November	December	January
Opening balance	0	1107.68	1085.36	1563.04
Sources of income:				
Regular- 3 days/week as FC	2600	2600	2600	2600
Additional days worked - bookkeeping	1200	600	600	600
Pension	350	350	350	350
Disabled child allowance	542	542	542	52
Other: affiliate marketing, sales of used items	380			
	5072	5199.68	5177.36	5165.04
Expenses:				
Mortgage	1122.33	1122.33	1122.33	1122.33
Hydro Electricity	150	150	150	150
Water	50	50	50	50
Property taxes	65	65	65	65
Heat pump finance	116	116	116	116
Car / Truck insurance	175	175	175	175
Cable, phone & internet	150	150	150	150
TV subscription	10.99	10.99	10.99	10.99
Medical	75	75	75	75
Gas	435	435	435	435
Groceries	865	865	865	865
Entertainment	100	100	100	100
Monthly savings	150	300	300	300
Christmas budget	500	500		
	3964.32	4114.32	3614.32	3614.32
Balance left over	1107.68	1085.36	1563.04	1550.72

This is nothing fancy and no skills are required to start one. As is plain to see – I STILL don't make a whole lot of money (but that's changing as we speak).

That being said, I can still afford my home, my car, to eat and to save on these meagre earnings.

I included my known, regular sources of income but I will update this monthly with additional sources of income as they arise and I will adjust the spend, save, invest categories accordingly.

I also like to maintain a checking account balance at around a stable $1500.

Do you know that the vast majority of people, the world over, have no idea where their money is going?

I know most of you aren't bookkeepers and some of you may even be afraid of numbers but I PROMISE you, this is simple, it's quick and it's free (If you have Microsoft office). I won't pay Microsoft a dime so I use Libreoffice (it's identical to Microsoft but it's free). Screw you Gates!

Most banks and credit card companies have the ability to allow a download of transactions for set periods in time (3 months, 6 months, etc). Chose [download CSV format]. This stands for Comma Separated Values and is ideal for plugging into a spreadsheet – just right click copy, right click paste :). Do this first! If your not familiar with computers, spreadsheets and downloads it may take you a while to get this done but the time and cost savings plus the additional free education you are now giving yourself for the future are INVALUABLE.

I am true to my word. Here's a Step by Step guide.

STEP 1: Sign in to your on-line banking

If you do not have online access then now is the time to register. Simply click the [register] button in the online portal and follow the instructions. Repeat for any financial institutions: banks, credit cards, etc.

Username or Access Card

+ Description (Optional)

Password

🔒 Login

Forgot your username or password?

STEP 2: Download your file

Once you have access to your account transactions there will be an option to download them with a drop down menu that allows more sophistication if you have an accounting

program. You don't need these programs. Simply choose the CSV file option. Make sure you choose 90 days of transactions (or more if that's an option).

You will now see a pop up that looks a little scary (text import..Account activity), just click OK.

STEP 3:

What happens next is a spreadsheet opens with your downloaded transactions!

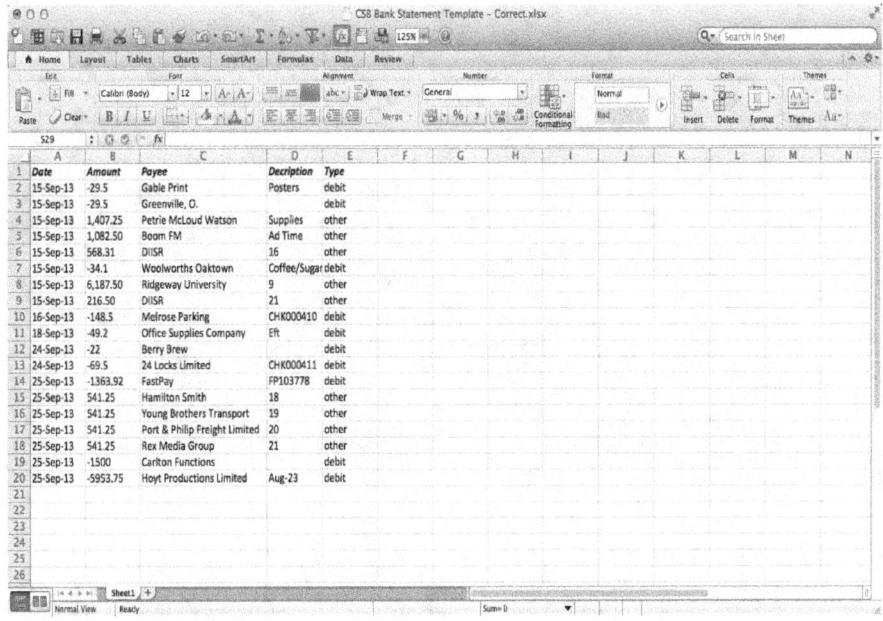

Once you have all of your accounts and transactions downloaded you can start to put them into a semblance of order. Start with your recurring payments like Mortgage or Rent, Bank fees, Hydro (Electricity). Note on which Day of each month these items leave the account. (Example is on Page 51).

STEP 4: (optional)

If you'd like a little spreadsheet lesson, here in step 4 we could Sort the Data.

Highlight the whole whole table from the first cell (A1) to the last cell. Go to the menu bar at the top of the computer screen and select DATA. From the drop down menu choose SORT.

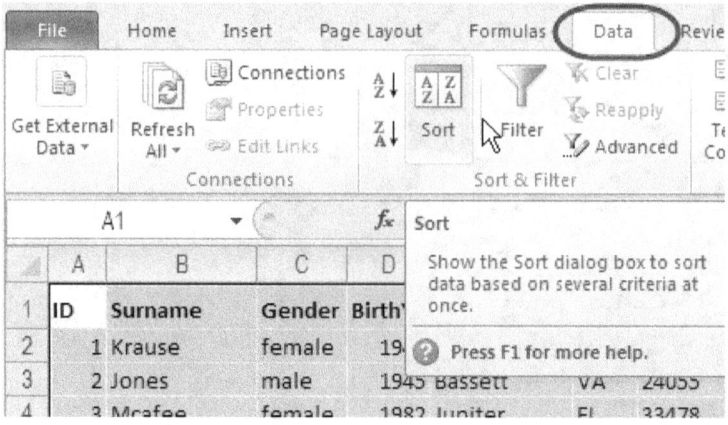

With this option you can choose to sort the data by NAME, Date, Amount or a combination. I would suggest we don't get fancy here. I like to leave my spreadsheet in date order because that's how my cash flow and budget is built.

If you are analyzing a years worth of data though it might be wise to sort by name so you can see recurring amounts more easily.

Step 5. Build out the spreadsheet

To build out the spreadsheet we will start adding columns. To add a column click on the next available (blank) column letter (C,D,E etc). This should highlight the column in blue. Right click for options and choose "insert column". I have the option in LibreOffice to Insert Columns Left or Right of the column I have highlighted but you may just have "Insert column". Name this column "TYPE". Go down the column and fill in what type of expense it is, eg Rent, Food, Phone, etc.

Here we could highlight the whole table again and [Data] [Sort] by "Type". This will allow you to total all the costs in the same categories and create a subtotal for each Spend Type.

Now you know what you have spent in one year in each category of expenditure. Once you have done this for each account and credit card you will know exactly where your money went.

What's your biggest number? Is it gas for the car? Debt repayments? Cash Withdrawals? The problem with cash withdrawals is that you have no idea what that money was spent on. It could have been a latte and magazine at lunchtime, a burger on the drive to somewhere, a journal for your daughter that caught your eye. That being said – Cash is about to become your new best friend.

Everyone in debt who has done any kind of research has heard of Dave Ramsey (right?) What about Gail Vaz-Oxlade (til debt do us part). Both of these Guru's advocate a cash based system when budgeting. Dave's is the Cash Envelope system and Gail's is the Glass jar system.

Simply put – you set up your jars (or envelopes) with your budgeted spend in cash for the week. If your grocery jar has $200 in it – that's all you have to spend on groceries. You do not take your debit or credit card out to the store with you and you calculate your spend as you go through the store doing your shopping.

Believe me, there is nothing in this world that will make you focus like knowing you have NOTHING EXTRA on you to pay the cashier at the end of your trip.

The beauty of the cash based system is that you can turn it into a game. If you budget to spend $200 but come in at $180 then transfer that "saved" $20 to a different jar. It should be Debt Repayment but it could be Fun Money or Holiday Gifts. You're the one living this life, not me.

Budgeting checklist

1. Make A List of ALL expenditure for a predefined period (1 year)
2. Open all your bills PROMPTLY
3. Schedule your payments according to when you get paid
4. Build / Review / Update your spreadsheets
5. Set up your Cash System
6. Find alternative sources of Income
7. Make a Plan to pay down Debt first

7.

The Art of False Economy

When Low Costs ~ Cost You.

Whether funds are limited or you're just committed to getting the most for your money, bargain shopping may not be your best bet all the times. I'm going to throw "Toilet paper" in here and you will all go "ah! - right". You see what I mean? A budget roll of toilet paper is wrapped loosely around the cardboard tube to appear as big as the non budget brand. The tube is also wider and the paper is thinner. You get far less for your money than it appears! Consider "More Bang for your Buck".

It's also usually worth considering the more expensive, higher-quality option when purchasing: Furniture; Shoes; Jeans; Classic clothing; Cookware; Appliances; Purses and Wallets; Luggage; Automobiles.

There are, of course, other categories in which it may pay to purchase the higher-end item. When in doubt, consider:

Replacement Costs.

When you're purchasing an item that could potentially last for years, consider durability as much as up-front cost. Buying one good pair of shoes for $150 can turn out to be a better investment than buying a $39 pair of shoes if the more expensive version lasts for years while the cheaper shoes have to be replaced in a few months.

Before making a purchase, think about how long you expect to need or want to use the item in question, and how much it would cost to replace it one or more times during that period.

Repair Costs

Saving money on a big ticket item like a refrigerator, or an even bigger ticket item like a vehicle, can mean premature replacement costs. But, even if you don't end up replacing the item, repair costs may eat up your savings and more.

When repairs are required, you're not only losing the benefit of the initial cost savings, but may incur additional costs—for example, you may miss work in order to wait for the repairman, or end up eating out for a few days while your oven or refrigerator is out of commission.

When making the initial cost comparison, consider both the condition of the item, reviews that indicate how durable it is and the length of the warranty you'll receive.

Other Associated Costs/Savings

When making your comparison, don't forget about indirect costs and savings. For example, when you purchase a high-end air filter, it may come with a permanent, washable filter—in other words, no ongoing costs. On the other hand, you may be able to purchase a much less expensive model, but have to order replacement filters every few months. Similarly, energy-efficient furnaces, refrigerators, washing machines and other equipment may cost more up front, but may lower ongoing utility costs and perhaps even qualify homeowners for rebates or tax credits.

The Bottom Line

The bottom line is that the bottom line is based on much more than the price tag. Think about durability and related costs before you make a decision, and you may well save money in the long run. And, as an added bonus, you just may find that you enjoy that higher quality product more than you would have the economy version.

8.

Food, Glorious Food!

Why is it so darned expensive?

Being able to stick to your budget is sure to translate to eating more at home rather than dining out a lot. Of course, it's a lot of fun to get out of the house and have a nice meal, but the cost to do so can add up quickly. Knowing the benefits of eating at home when you're watching your budget may have you leaning more in this direction when it comes to appeasing your appetite.

Saving Money

Dining at home is sure to be cheaper than going out for a meal in most cases. You may find some good deals at various locations, but overall if you want to pay less, you should eat at home. The average cost of a meal for just two people at sit down restaurant can be as much as $50-$75 and this may not even include having an alcoholic beverage or two. This can really add up if you dine out too much and this is yet another reason to avoid eating out a great deal.

Controlling your Weight

It can be a real challenge to maintain your weight if you eat outside of the home a lot. This is because of the extra ingredients that are put into your food when it's prepared by others.

Dining out means you will be unable to control the fat, sugar or preservatives that are added to your food. This can quickly translate to weight gain and could even mean potential health problems for you in the future. If you sincerely want to control your weight, it's ideal to eat at home rather than when you're out and about or on the road.

Less Hassle!

It's nice to have a special dinner planned with family and loved ones or to savour the taste of a gourmet meal, but all of this requires preparation. You'll need to get dressed up; plan the place you want to visit and even drive there and then there's the cost of the meal.

It's just so much easier to eat at home, have everyone bring a dish and avoid the traffic and hassle of leaving the house sometimes! There are also benefits to dining out too and you're sure to want to make the most of these at times so it should be reserved for a really special occasion. Quality over Quantity would be my "Go To" here. The key to saving money, losing weight or maintaining it is as simple as eating at home.

Paying Off Credit Cards

You will have a better chance of paying off your credit cards sooner if you dine at home more. You can put the money you would be spending at the restaurants onto your monthly payments, and this is sure to be the best way to help you get this paid off. One of the best things you can do is get your credit card debt paid down because of the high-interest rates that are associated with these cards. The key to being able to do so is to spend less money and put your entire extra money towards getting the debt paid down.

In short ~ Don't Dine Out

Everyone loves going out to eat or ordering some delicious Chinese takeout. The problem is it can get very pricey, you could spend up to 400 dollars on dining out in just one month alone. This would be on top of your grocery money! Instead of going out to eat start shopping once or twice a month.

If you go to the grocery store you can spend 200 dollars and eat for two weeks (sometimes more). It may take you a while to get a good food shopping system in place but once you do it is easy to see how you cut back on your spending.

Best Ways to Manage Food Budget

Upon reviewing your bank statements, it is likely that you will be shocked at how much money you spend on food / dining / eating out. Most people don't know where to begin when they think of food budgeting. Should I stop going out to eat? Should I plan all of my meals? There are many techniques to lower your monthly food costs. It may mean you will have to make your own meals, or will have to limit the amount you eat at restaurants. But when you have an extra few hundred bucks in your bank, there is no doubt you'll be grateful for having made this budget!

Here are some tips for managing your own food budget:
1. Don't go to the grocery store all the time. Grocery stores are full of temptations. You'll see a million things you want, and you are bound to end up purchasing some items you don't need.

2. Remembering not to shop while hungry is also a useful tip that goes hand in hand with not visiting the grocery store often. You'll make better decisions about your food purchases when you go on a full stomach.

3. Pay attention to the sales and see what looks fresh.

4. Use a grocery list. When you do go to the store, you should have a list of items you're looking for. This will limit the amount of time you spend wandering, so you will only get what you truly need. A good way to keep track of what you need is to have an ongoing grocery store list on the table. Staples like bananas, coffee, milk, and bread need to be watched, as these tend to run out the quickest. As soon as you notice you're getting low, put it on your list.

5. Meal plans are your friend. This means you should be planning out your meals every week. You'll have chicken and green beans on Monday, for instance, and pizza on Tuesday. That way, you can keep track of what you're eating and spending. If you want more freedom, you don't have to have set days for these meals. If they're frozen or nonperishable, you can have these meals whenever you want, and this will give you some options.

6. Utilize grocery store flyers. This will keep you informed on what is affordable this week and it will also help you plan meals. If chicken is one sale, for instance, you can include chicken in your meal for the week. Or if other ingredients are on sale, you can look up recipes online for inspiration.

Meal Planning and Meal Prep in a little more detail.

Have you seen Pinterest? It's an online, visual search engine.

If one where to go online to Pinterest and type in "Meal Plans" a veritable plethora of "Pins" will be thrown in front of your eyes. Sounds painful but it's actually a little addictive.

Simply click on one of the wonderful images and you will be led to a site that gives you the ingredients required and step by step tutorials for the preparation of whatever wonderful concoction took your fancy.

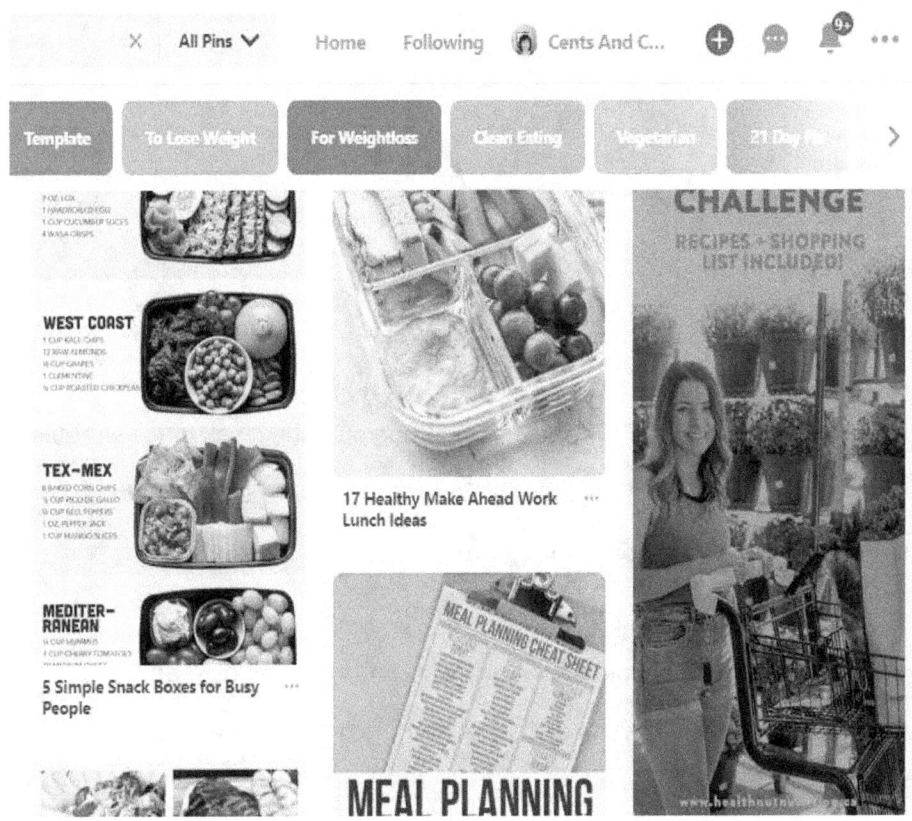

You can further refine the search to focus on Vegetarian or Keto, etc.

You can start with a plain old notepad or, get a bit fancy and download a printable Meal Planner and Grocery List like this one:-

If you head over to my Blog site and sign up you get access to the Freebie Vault that has this downloadable PDF plus LOTS more great stuff!

www.spendaholicsanonymous.com

Now – we tend to meal plan as a family on Friday evenings – after the weekly budgets have been established and before the ritual Pizza and movie night commences.

Every Friday night my husband and I will update the bank records and the budget, review the upcoming bills and allocate the funds to our glass jars accordingly. (Even after so long we still use Gail Vaz-Oxlades jars system).

It's easier to plan meals for the week if the kids are involved. This way we also have buy in and limited sabotage. We have a list of our favourites: Spaghetti; Pizza Chicken (Parmigiana); Taco's; Shepherds Pie; Chicken Chow Mein; Chinese curry & Rice, etc, etc. The list is quite long actually which makes choosing a varied week (from the previous week) really easy. Breakfasts are easy because we keep several things on hand: waffles, cereal, toast. We are allowed to choose our own breakfast from the "designated breakfast items". I have to stipulate this as I have a teenage boy who see's nothing wrong with a meatball sub for breakfast!

Once the plan is made my husband (the Chef) then prepares the grocery shopping list for the plan and adding any household items required, such as detergent, etc. He ALWAYS performs a house inventory first!
My job is to then take the list and "shop" the flyers finding deals and bargains wherever possible.
Between the two of us we have our Saturday morning plan of action! Normally my husband will shop alone (I'm the one with the spending problem) but, when we do go together, I take my "allowance" with me so I'm not using grocery money for a pretty journal, etc.

If we find an offer for a bulk purchase then, once we get home, the "excess" is portioned off into freezer bags and moved out to the auxiliary freezer in the workshop. The reason for this is – if it's not in the house itself my kids won't go out to the shop to look for it!

Are you ready for some Extreme grocery money saving ideas?

I know not everyone can live on a rural half acre like I do but everyone can have Patio Plants in pots or a small garden / greenhouse. A pack of seeds costs less than a head of lettuce and provides fresh greens for 70% of the year. I grew fresh lettuce in a plastic tote on my back deck one year. I have grown patio tomatoes and zucchinis in pots. I have strawberry hanging baskets (instead of flowers) on my front porch. There's nothing as rewarding as picking a fresh tomato off your plant for lunch.

Today – I supplement our grocery bill with full time growing in the garden. We never buy raspberries, blueberries or strawberries from the store because I have an abundance of them in the garden. I don't buy cherries, apples or pears... I have trees. I plan my garden each year to grow what we use – Potatoes, onions, garlic, carrots, beets. Occasionally I get creative with something exotic but...we don't eat that way so usually it's a waste of space and energy!

We keep four or five chickens. Eggs a plenty! (Please check your local ordinance rules before considering this). Not allowed chickens? What about Quail? Smaller, quieter and keeping ten quail is no more hassle than keeping two.

Do you hunt? Can you fish? I'm fortunate enough to live on an island in British Columbia where the opportunity to hunt and fish is plenty, and we take full advantage of this opportunity.

I briefly touched on the subject earlier of preserving food. Lets say you have no intention of even growing a little bit of salad for yourself but you do find a humoungous sack of carrots on the "disaster rack" (produce being sold off extremely cheaply). Having something as simple as canning jars and a pressure caner means those carrots can now be processed to last up to one whole year on your pantry shelf. Those leftover berries in your freezer from the summer can become jams, preserves, pie fillings and, if not eaten, given as gifts. (Two birds with one stone!)
I "purchased" my caner at a yard sale for $15 and I get my mason jars from the thrift store or from online local sales.

Preserving food can be tricky and I would always recommend you get help from someone who knows what they are doing or follow the instructions on your caner and from a food preservation book carefully. Botulism is not something to take lightly. That being said, I've canned everything from apples to hot dogs (not recommended) and nothing bad has happened.

Don't want to risk pressure caning? What about dehydrating food or making your own bread? I picked up two dehydrators, a bread machine and a yogurt making machine from my local online forum and all together paid less than $100. Of course, you don't need a bread machine to make your own bread but.. it sure is easier, faster and less messy! My bread machine was Five Bucks and came with a recipe book! Think about how many bread products you buy in a week versus the flour and yeast to make your own? An added bonus is that you can set the machine at bedtime and wake up to a freshly baked loaf....mmmm!

Economies of Scale

You may remember this from school but, buying larger quantities, or buying in bulk, costs less and saves more in the long run. Buying food in bulk wastes money if your not able to preserve it or use it. What's the point in buying ten kilos of Avocado's on sale? You can't "can" Avocado (or Guacamole for that matter) and you won't be able to use them all up before they rot.

So – why do I advocate stockpiling?

Non perishables bought today will never be this cheap again. Next month the price of those things will have increased. Anyone remember Dollar Days, Dolarama, Poundland? Not so long ago our stores would sell things for $1 (dollar days). Now those days are Dollar Ninety Nine Days. You see, inflation is inevitable and, in the last decade, nothing has increased in price as much as food.
So – Stockpiling....Don't Freak Out! I'm not talking Doomsday Preppers here!

Pay attention to the grocery store flyers and sales. When toilet roll or coffee go on sale, buy as much as you can afford and put it away. Shopping in your personal store in one months time for shampoo or toothpaste that you paid half price for four weeks ago makes more economic sense than buying it again today at full price, doesn't it?

I may have mentioned it already (or not) but I have an extremely Faddy personality. I latch onto to something (like book binding, bullet journalling or making bath products) for a couple of weeks at a time and then, I'm done. Don't want to do that any more. Not so with the stockpiling. I still do this today and it's super satisfying.

Our story..
During the first year of making our comeback we never purchased a single roll of toilet paper, bottle of shampoo, tube of toothpaste or can of coffee from a store. This is because, when we were earning Mega Bucks I was stockpiling at each sale. At every grocery shop I would add just one or two more things to my personal stores at home and, it literally saved us.
I still do this today. My current project is "Operation College".
I have a tote that I put $10 worth of products into each week for my daughter to take to school. She has a grocery budget of $100 per week and I know, on those weeks that she has to resupply her toiletries or paper products, she be eating Ramen! My hope is that, whilst living off a very meagre budget she learns to appreciate having an emergency supply as back up. Also super useful if we have a zombie invasion!

9.

Tricks for Stopping Your Overspending Habit

Overspending has become a huge problem in today's fast paced world. People tend to spend way more money than they have, and often find themselves in debt over it. When you overspend you not only stress yourself out, but the people around you.

It can take some time and a lot of practice but if you put the work forward you can make sure that overspending isn't a problem for you. There are plenty of neat tricks and tips you can keep in mind to keep your budget in line. Here are 3 great ways to make sure you never have to stress about overspending again.

Spend Wisely

Many people find themselves in situations where they want to spend money so they can look and feel good. The problem with buying everything you want, as opposed to what you need, is that often you dig yourself a hole.

I'm a prime example of this!

One of the best things you can do is to think carefully about what you are going to buy before you buy it.

Take a couple of seconds to recognize whether you are impulse spending or just buying something that you actually need. If you start buying wants instead of needs you will find yourself overspending in a hurry.

Pro Tip – walk away. If you come back a few days later and the item is still available and you have evaluated the Wants .v. Needs scenario, then by all means, get it.

Never Carry All of Your Money with You

It might sound kind of silly at first, but if you carry all of your money with you the odds are you are going to overspend. There are a couple places you can keep your extra funds, such as a bank or in a hidden spot in your home. You will be surprised at how much less you spend if you do not have all of your money available at once. Act as if the only money you have is what it in your pocket at that particular time, even if you have thousands in your safe at home (lol).

Avoid Credit Cards

Credit cards are used by people all over the world to help them solve their debt problem.

The truth is it will not only make your debt problem worse, but will cause you to overspend more than you would otherwise. There are plenty of reasons you should avoid credit cards such as:

- Insane interest rates
- Monthly fees and subscriptions
- An extra bill every month

If you find that you need a credit card to make ends meet then you are not alone but this is the <u>Main Area</u> we need to fix. If you find yourself in this situation, make sure to follow trick one and spend your funds wisely. If you follow these tips you will be a step closer to avoiding overspending.
Will this take a little getting use to? Sure, it might – depending on how crazy you were with the budget, or lack of budget, before today. However, if you stick with it and make sure that you are keeping your goal in sight, you should have no problem stopping your bad habit of overspending. Before you know it, you might become one of those people who get a thrill out of saving money instead.

Tips for Determining How to Cut Back On Your Spending

Spending money is something that cannot be avoided no matter who you are or where you are from. At some point you are going to need some spending cash, and in some cases you might be stuck because you do not have any extra spending cash. If this is a problem for you here are some tips to determine how to cut back on your spending and get ahead.

Check Your Bills ~ *validate the charges*

Sit down one day and really look at all of your bills. Maybe you will notice something that you overlooked, such as your out of hand $140 a month house phone bill. When you see something like high priced bills come up with an alternative solution to save some money.

Back to the $140 house phone, are you paying for a cell phone too? If the answer to that question is yes, then you could always get your house phone turned off. This scenario is providing everyone in your household has a cell phone, or you live alone. If you switch to just your cell phone you will instantly see savings from dropping that particular bill.

Of course, in my story we all had cell phones and I went with keeping the Landline phone (part of a discounted bundle package with internet) and getting rid of the cell phones. GASP!

The amount of people who almost die of shock when we say we don't have cell phones is laughable. It's better when it's my 18 year old daughter. Her friends think she's an abused child!

Do you know what – no one died. We continued life without cell phones, even today.

Keep Invoices and Receipts

Most of the time if you go to a store and someone offers you your receipt you may just tell them to throw it out. Make sure you start taking those receipts! You should always keep receipts from things like:

Paying Bills

Gas station

Department stores

ANYTHING purchased with Cash!!

The reason it is important to hold onto this information is because neither people nor technology is perfect. Mistakes are made more often than you might imagine. When you finally get home at the end of the day look over your invoices and receipts to make sure everything is correct.

Sometimes there can be overcharges where you end up paying much more, but simply didn't realize when you paid. If you contact these people after the fact you can get some of your money back which leads to better budgeting.

With all of the previously mentioned tips in mind, you should have absolutely no trouble in making sure that you are able to cut back on your spending. Sure, you might find it a little difficult at first, especially if you have been someone that has overspent for many years. However, as with anything, practice will make perfect and you will be able to stick to a clean cut budget in no time at all.

Ways to Lower your Monthly Bills

Keeping your monthly bills down is very important for your financial well-being. The key to doing this is taking the time to find ways to cut your costs. This may not be the most enjoyable task because you may be forced to do away with some of the luxury items in your life. However, knowing ways to lower your monthly bills is critical to your success.

Turn off the Cable

Do you really need to have hundreds of channels to watch when you only watch a couple? One of the biggest ways you can waste your money is by investing a good hunk of your paycheck into the cable TV package. You probably don't watch as much television as you think because of working and doing other things through the week. So, you can reduce your monthly costs by disconnecting the cable in your home. The average price of having this service can be as high as $100 and up, depending on your package.

In order to stave off a rebellion we actually invested $20 a month on Netflix and Crave TV. There's no shortage of crap to watch and no one is calling Child Line or being hauled off to family court!

Join a Health Club

Getting out of the house to eat out, shop or see a movie costs money every time you go.

A great alternative (and investment) is to join a health club and visit as frequently as you like. You can save money over time, and this will allow you to get healthier and engage in an activity that you enjoy frequently. It also gets you away from the TV and those Cable bills, right?

Be sure to check around your local area to find the place you would like to visit often and that offers the best possible price. This is an ideal way to help you stay entertained, active and save money all at the same time.

See if you can assume membership from someone who is giving theirs up or moving out of town. Always inquire about a months free trial too before you sign up. That way you will know if it's the right fit for you. Occasionally there are sales through companies like Groupon. Excellent cost savings can be made by taking advantage of a sale or membership drive.

Drive Less

Do your really have to jump in the car for every trip you make? The chances are you may be able to walk a lot of places and avoid even starting your vehicle and using the gasoline that comes with doing this. Consider walking to the store or across the street every chance that you get and you will be able to see you gasoline costs decrease and even your weight for that matter.

You can save money on a regular basis when you find effective ways to allow this to happen. It's necessary to do your research and work towards decreasing your monthly costs as much as possible when you can to help save money.

Our story...

We've always had two vehicles but, when it came down to it, with only one of us working, we decided to pool resources and take one vehicle off the road. In doing this we saved $102 a month on the insurance and approx $40 a week on Gas. No unnecessary trips are taken and our routes are planned to minimize the journey and maximize the cost savings.

Our typical morning run would be:- drop boy child at high School (8:30am); drop Mom at office (8:50am); drop girl child at part time job (9:15am); home by 10:00am. The added advantage of this for me is I have my own personal chauffeur! I haven't really found a disadvantage yet.

Tips for Saving Money on your Electric Bill

Being able to keep your electric bill under control in severely cold or hot weather is important. If the summer season is here, this means your AC unit is sure to be running a great deal. This can increase your energy costs, but knowing ways to offset these costs will still allow you to stay cool and keep your monthly bill within your reach.

Use the Ceiling Fan

One of the best ways to keep the air flowing in your home without making your electricity bill drastically increase is by relying more on your ceiling fan. This will assist you in being able to stay cooler with it running regardless of what the temperature outside may be.

If you don't currently have a ceiling fan installed, you will want to be sure to put one of these in your home to reduce your energy costs as much as possible.

Change the Air Filter

HVAC experts recommend that you change the air filter in your home at least once every three months. This will allow the air coming out of the vents to be much cooler than if you had dirty and clogged filter in place. Your unit simply won't run as efficiently if you have old filters in place. It's ideal to change these as necessary, and this is an inexpensive way for you to work towards keeping your energy bills down.

Watch the Thermostat

Simply keeping the temperature in your home a little higher than it needs to be during the months of summer is an ideal way for you to keep your costs down. Studies indicate that raising the temperature in your home only two degrees can significantly lower your energy costs and these savings can add up quickly. Let's face it – you're not going to die if your a degree or two warmer.

Consider investing in a programmable thermostat that will only allow the AC to turn on when you're away from home if you have it set to do so. This is a great way for you to reduce all of your energy costs during the summer. Additionally, you will be able to come home to a cool home after you've been gone for a while.

Turn off the Lights

If you're not using lights in a certain room, be sure to turn these off when you leave the room. Many people are aware that leaving the lights on for a short amount of time isn't too costly, but over time all of these costs will add up on your bill.

You may want to consider getting efficient energy bulbs, as well. These have been proven to help save you money on many of your energy costs and are ideal for any room of your home.

By taking the time and making the effort, you're sure to find some ways that can be helpful in reducing your energy costs a great deal. Once you monthly electric bills are noticeably lower, this will motivate you to continue to work to reduce energy costs.

11.

Your Credit Score

What's your number? Do you know what your credit score is? Do you know if your score is good or bad?

It's ludicrous to note that most people have no idea what their credit score is or how it affects them. This is easy to fix. I use a service called CreditKarma.ca which is free to use. When you go to the site it allows you to input some details and then shows you your score:-

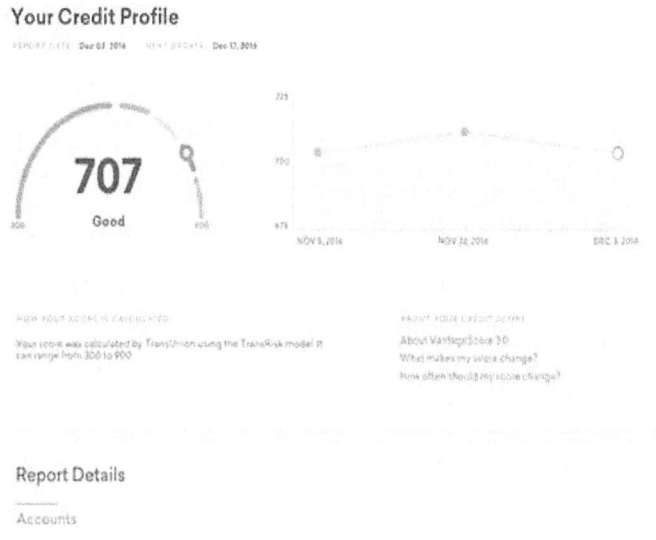

There are two credit bureaus in Canada and they are responsible for tracking your use of credit and providing potential lenders with information about your financial health that will allow the lender to make an informed decision to give you more credit or a loan or mortgage ~ Transunion and Equifax.

The bad news here is that neither of these bureaus have a responsibility to ensure the information that they hold about you is correct.
SAY WHAT??

Both agencies are legally obligated to mail you your report free of charge after you fill out the request (average wait time 21 to 28 days). Most people will pay the online fee to have access to their information immediately. That's why I love CreditKarma.ca – it's free and I can see what I need to see immediately.

Our story...
When we first married and in the market for a mortgage we found out that my husband had a bankruptcy on his file. Needless to say it wasn't his but, with the exact same name and date of birth being shown for the bankrupt person, it was an uphill battle for us to prove it wasn't him. This culminated in a sworn affidavit at the notaries office, which was not cheap!
Mistakes get made – especially by humans.

At one time (in the dark days of my long forgotten life in England) I used to have a "catalogue" account. Upon moving house I called to change my address on the account and the clerk taking the details missed the "S" from MRS as she typed in my new details. As both hubster and I have the same first initial and last name, my account became his and the company refused to speak with me without first having HIS permission to do so! I was livid, especially since this was an account for Christmas things that I was hiding from him at the time.

What factors determine your score?

Let me just say here that having No Credit is as damaging as having too much or bad credit! Lenders need something to look at if they are to make a decision about you.

Number one is your payment history. The more loans or cards you have being reported as "paid on time", the better your credit score will be. Accounts paid late lower your score and having a public record of collections, including wage garnishments, liens or judgments (Consumer Proposal or Bankruptcy) will significantly hurt your credit score. This doesn't last forever though and it is possible to improve your score, even after a Consumer Proposal.

Next in line is "The Amounts you Owe". We call this Credit utilization. If you are constantly maxed out on your credit cards you are a greater credit risk than someone who pays in full or keeps balances minimum. Lenders ADORE people who don't actually need the money it seems! Having large balances available to you and requesting a new loan or card is also a red flag. Lenders would be wary of you suddenly using all of the credit available to you which reduces the likelihood of them being paid back. Number three is the length of time you have used credit. If you can demonstrate a long history of using credit wisely then the better off your score will be. When looking at this category a lender will look at how long you've had your oldest account, when did you last get a new type of credit account, what is your average credit life and how long has it been since you used your available lines of credit or cards.

Number three – New Credit. The greatest risk to a lender is someone who opens up several new accounts in a short space of time. What's going on here? How many accounts do you have? When did you last open an account? How many requests for credit have you made? This doesn't include shopping around for rates and typically you are not penalized for this.

Your score will typically not be effected by similar types of credit inquiries made in the same 30 to 45 day period so, all your credit card inquiries in the 30 days leading up to your report are classed as one credit inquiry.

Lastly, your lenders will look at what types of credit are in use. Credit cards and store accounts would be revolving credit and car loans would be fixed credit. Do you have all revolving credit or is here a mix of types? Ask me why this matters and I have to say I have no idea!

Why does having a good credit score matter?

When you are the lowest risk customer (the best kind a lender could want) you can command the best deals; the lowest interest rates, more credit offers than you need, a choice of high quality lenders and this could also get you into the worse kind of trouble. With lenders falling all over themselves to have you in their stable it would be easy to stock up and max out. The road to soul crushing debt doesn't happen when you're broke. It happens when you have money and are offered lots of lovely money for more lovely stuff and then suddenly, the minimum payments are more than you can afford to make. Just because you can get your hands on more debt doesn't mean you should. Your score doesn't say you can afford the debt, it just guesses at whether you will pay it off or not (default)

Our story...

Two mature adults with a long history a using credit wisely. Six figure household income. 2.2 children and a white picket fence...sign here.

Fast forward to one cold and dreary day at the end of January – just as the Christmas Credit card statements are due to be paid and POOF! Jobs gone.

Monthly income now goes from $4500 to just over $2000 but the bills remain the same.

Our lenders looked at our scores and were very pleased but never looked at our Income to debt levels and at what might happen if those income levels were halved.

In our 20 years of marriage we have managed to score two, maybe three consolidation loans and then...racked the debt straight back up again. The number one rule of taking a debt consolidation is <u>DO NOT UTILIZE THE CARDS OR LINES YOU JUST CLEARED WITH THE LOAN</u>! (and you sure as hell don't do it two or three times). Your first "Needed" consolidation loan is your red flag and your get out of jail free card. Heed the warning.

Here are some of the tricks we have used to rebuild our credit following a Consumer Proposal.

Get a credit card specifically aimed at people rebuilding their credit. Capital One is our choice. They have lots of options and are generally very forgiving.

Make the minimum payments on time – *at the VERY least*. At this stage I would say, if you're rebuilding your credit, keep the credit limit low and use it sparingly – paying the balance in full each time.

Never go over 50% of your available credit and actually 30% is my preferred number!

Don't do it AT ALL if you can't afford it!

Be wary about using credit. I just received my first card since our proposal (almost three years) and It terrified me. My first purchase was $1.34 and I paid it back in full before my statement came through. Here's another thing...paying your balance early used to mean it didn't register on your credit score as a positive but now it shows your utilization in a better light. This can all be very confusing and I recommend reading ValuePenguin.com. It's a mine of useful information on all things credit card related.

12.

Gaining control over your Money

Does the thought of having to track every single penny of expenditure from here on in depress you? Are you afraid that once you tale a long hard look at where your money goes you might just give up before you even start? There are some that would advocate for not doing this (tracking expenditures) because depression is a serious condition. Stress is also serious and the suffocating feeling of being crushed by debt is one all too familiar by too many people. What about sleep deprivation? Used in Wars as a form of torture? When you put yourself through this (and possibly your Spouse too) you are actually inflicting a form of torture on yourself.

My thoughts on the subject are simple. Are you in debt? Do you want to get out? Then Man Up.
You can't get out if you don't know how you got in (or are in denial about how you got there).
If you don't fancy keeping all your receipts and tracking cash purchases then download an App. There's an App for everything these days. Understanding your spending habits is the first step to freeing yourself.

Once we realized how frivolous we were with money and once we made a budget that we could stick to, it freed us up enough to realize that we could afford our lifestyle working only part time. I now work three days a week instead of five (previously seven!) and, let me tell you, having a four day weekend every week is mind blowing!

13.

Making more ~ The Art of the Side Hustle

Whats a Side Hustle? Glad you asked.

A side hustle is simply today's phrase for earning a little extra cash on the side (outside of your regular work).

When I decided to go Part time with work it was essentially to become a part time blogger too. I had visions of being one of these 6 or 7 figure earners by spewing my wisdom a couple of times a week to my adoring readers.

Everyone needs a dream right? Lying on a beach with a shiny Mac telling people how I managed to afford my luscious lifestyle whilst not having an actual JOB! Today – I'm more likely to be found in the garden with dirt under my nails than on a beach but, I do blog, that's a thing, and I do make a little side money from it now... not enough to retire but hey!

I do a little affiliate marketing on my website (selling other peoples goods through links) for which I earn a small commission. I never promote something I don't have, want or use. Integrity is key.

I take part in Email and Facebook marketing using Sales Funnels. That's a whole book in itself and takes a great deal of skill and time to build an audience that is large enough to earn you decent money. Who read your emails and who trust you not to push any ole crap at them just to make a buck.

I also take on extra bookkeeping work before Christmas or if I want to make a larger than normal purchase.

I now look at things with a "How can I afford"…rather than saying I can't afford.

Another great way to get out of debt is to look at Passive Income. This is money you make 24 – 7, even while you sleep. It can come in the form of dividends from investments or book sales or courses and printables that are offered for sale through your website, etc.

If you need ideas on Side Hustles or Passive Income: Google or Pinterest. The Net is chock full of people spouting their greatness and mastery and for just $197/ $999 / $2479 you too can learn what they know. Some of this information is valuable and will definitely put you on the right path but the majority is garbage. Do your research. Read reviews. Google the name of the course + Scam and see what pops up. You might be surprised.

14.

The State of the Nation

Why is the consumer debt crisis so bad? I blame advertising. We all want more stuff, good stuff, fancy stuff. Bigger, Better, Faster, Louder.

There used to be two seasons in the fashion industry (Spring/Summer and Fall/Winter), then that moved to four with the actual seasons. Now there are 52 seasons in each year. The stores need you to buy something new each and every week and I used to be one of those girls that didn't go out on a Saturday night without something new to wear.

Technology moves so fast that you no sooner leave a store with the latest Gizmo and a week later the pre launch for the next model has started..flatter screen, better camera, more pixels, less shake, more rattle, less roll...whatever.

The price for raw materials keeps rising and so the cost of living increases but the wages you make don't move...sometimes for years at a time. We want a high standard of living and so we turn to debt to get us the things we want.

Spending more than you make or living beyond your means is a recipe for disaster and yet over 90% of North Americans live this way. Have you heard the term "Good Debt"?

Don't be ridiculous. There's no such thing as Good Debt.
Some would argue that student loan debt is good debt and I ask why? You leave school with a crushing amount of debt and no way to pay it back and it follows you around during your early adult years like a noose around your neck. What's good about that?
Many enter into marriage still carrying student debt and if that's both of you, good luck getting a mortgage.

With more and more students leaving college and Uni with degrees that costs hundreds of thousands of dollars to obtain and more and more jobs being eroded or replaced by AI, leaving the remaining jobs being a highly sought after prize and often not paying the expected rate for a new Grad, the "Free World" as we know it is headed for a shit storm of epic proportions.

With the onslaught of new technology we have become the Instant Gratification era. Go online, free shipping, get in in 24 hours, no need to leave the armchair or for pants to be worn. What's not to love?

I grew up impoverished and that did not teach me respect for money. Once I earned my own money I spent it like there was no tomorrow. I know people who grew up affluent and they squeak when they walk they're so tight (when it comes to money).

I sought approval from friends by having nice things, getting acknowledged by the "IT" girls for wearing the latest fashion, having my opinions listened to because I was paying for the soda's and that mentality came with me into my adult years.

We've become a society that limits people who don't have credit. Want to check into a hotel? Not without a credit card you don't. Want to rent a car – credit card required. Need a mortgage? Nope – no credit history means we don't know if we can trust you or not. Whatever happened to the house as the collateral?

It's so easy to get credit today (and it's been toughened up a lot in recent years). That it should scare us, but it doesn't.
I have bad credit (super low FICO score). A consumer proposal is registered on my file. I applied for a card to rebuild my credit and my new starting limit????
$4000.
Seriously. W.T.F??

I held that card in my hand and visions of new MacBooks and vacations sprang so easily to mind that I started to shake. I then gave the card to my husband and told him to put it way. I know I can spend $4k in one weekend and I wouldn't break a sweat.

I know it could take me almost five years to find the money to pay that balance back at my current earning levels. This would mean I would have to go back to work full time again.

It just wasn't worth it to me. My freedom for some stuff? Or we could use the money and fly off to an island and sit by the sea for a week doing nothing. Well, I live on an Island and by the sea and for four days a week I could do nothing if I so choose. Doesn't that seem ridiculous when you lay it out that way?

Have you played Monopoly lately? I play with my son and he is a mixed bag. Land in jail? He's rather pay $50 and get out immediately than waste a few turns trying to roll a double. Play Rich Dad, Poor Dad "Cashflow" and he ends up Mayor of his City and sitting pretty. He usually wins at Monopoly too by the way, but his strategy is fool proof. He collects the crappy properties straight after Go.. all of them. Everyone of us lands on those properties each time we go around the board and no amount of $200 for passing Go can save you in a long game. My son always plays the Long Game!

If you ask him what he wants to be when he leaves High School and his answer is Billionaire, Philanthropist, Playboy (too much Tony stark?). I have pointed out that we may hit a snag when it comes to work experience but hey, I love his thinking.

I firmly believe that debt is a disease and consumerism an addiction and I'm hoping I have demonstrated (to my kids if not to you), that it doesn't have to stay that way. Downsize your house (and mortgage). Figure out how to live on one income while you can still make two (if you have a partner, of course). Choose less and enjoy more. Embrace minimalism!

Head over to **www.spendaholicsanoymous.com** and sign up for the 12 Step program. Just like an AA program, if you follow the steps you will break free and, just like AA, if you relapse, pick yourself up and start again. We don't judge!
People who have lived in glass houses learn NEVER to throw stones.

Start taking care of you and yours NOW because the next crisis might be right around the corner.

Resources

Credit counselling

www.4pillars.com
www.creditcanada.com

Credit bureaus

www.transunion.ca
www.equifax.ca

www.creditkarma.ca

Blog sites

www.spendaholicsanonymous.com
www.valuepenguin.com

www.easysafemoney.com

Books

Rich Dad, Poor Dad – Robert Kiyosaki
Til Debt do us part – Gail Vaz-Oxlade
The Science of getting rich – Wallace D Wattles
E scape – Anik Singal

Other

www.debtclock.ca
www.Usdebtclock.org
www.capitalone.ca
www.statscanada.ca
www.pinterest.ca

LibreOffice – free spreadsheets

www.ingramcontent.com/pod-product-compliance
Lightning Source LLC
Chambersburg PA
CBHW071406220526
45469CB00004B/1182